Heàling

RICARDO TRINIDAD

BOOK SERIES BY FIG FACTOR MEDIA

WordPower Book Series

© Copyright 2021, Fig Factor Media, LLC.
All rights reserved.

All rights reserved. No portion of this book may be reproduced by mechanical, photographic or electronic process, nor may it be stored in a retrieval system, transmitted in any form or otherwise be copied for public use or private use without written permission of the copyright owner.

It is sold with the understanding that the publisher and the individual authors are not engaged in the rendering of psychological, legal, accounting or other professional advice. The content and views in each chapter are the sole expression and opinion of its author and not necessarily the views of Fig Factor Media, LLC.

For more information, contact:

Fig Factor Media, LLC | www.figfactormedia.com

Cover Design & Layout by Juan Pablo Ruiz
Printed in the United States of America

ISBN: 978-1-957058-04-7
Library of Congress Control Number: 2021923566

DEDICATION

I dedicate this to all those in need of healing and to let you know you are not alone.

ACKNOWLEDGMENTS

I would like this opportunity to acknowledge Ruth Vallejo who has helped me to focus on my health and fitness. Thank you and I love you. I would also like to say thank you to my team of amazing people that have worked on energy healing and helping me get rid of old trauma including Sunni Boehme, Ether Okear, Darcy Mason, and Curry Chowder Chaudoir. Finally, I would like to thank Jackie Camacho for her vision in this book.

INTRO

Many words describe the successful entrepreneur, but Healing can be easily overlooked. Entrepreneurs tend to have a bulletproof mentality. There is so much to do and so little time that health takes a back seat to business, family, and community. Trips to the gym become fewer, fast food becomes part of the shortcut to success. Other words that describe entrepreneurs might be: overweight, sleep-deprived, pasty, and irritable.

My journey always included exercise but along the way I focused more on sales, profits, web sites, and more customers. I was completely stressed out. Then, out of the blue came a diagnosis: prostate cancer. Going through cancer made me focus on healing. Since then, I've stayed healthy, limber, and strong. Getting back on track with health has made me better at running my company. I have more energy and focus. My goal is to enjoy my life and stay away from doctors. In this book, I list my favorite health hacks: how I keep body, mind and spirit soaring.

MEDITATION

Breathwork is how I start every day. There are so many guided and non-guided meditations, but I find writing down my own intentions and saying them in a meditative state helps to bring about the life I want to focus on. I start with 10-20 minutes of breath work to put myself in an awake but relaxed mode which is the best way to meditate. I meditate three times a day on gratitude, love, health, and prosperity.

Looking for help with breath work and meditation? Check out Wim Hof's breathwork and the Silva Method on YouTube. My Tip: Say your meditation through your heart center.

EXERCISE

We all been told how important exercise is but it's crucial for the entrepreneur who spends hours behind a desk. Keeping your heart and core muscles in good shape will keep you out of the doctor's office and give you the energy you need to succeed. Staying with a workout plan of at least 3-4 times a week is probably the hardest part. I change up exercise times to include High Intensity Interval Training (HIIT) using lighter weights and higher reps, walking several miles, and yoga. Yoga is really great for your mind and body. My Tip: try hot yoga which is done in a heated room.

EARTHING/GROUNDING

Earthing or grounding is so amazing for your health, and it doesn't require much. Earthing means to be connected to the Earth. Simply walking or sitting barefoot in your backyard is connecting you to the Earth's energy. Since the introduction of plastic and rubber-soled shoes, we have become disconnected from the Earth's energy. The Earth's Energy is healing and one that every plant and animal relies on. Earthing can improve sleep, stop snoring, and help heal or improve chronic inflammation, immune system, wound repair, white blood cells, macrophages, and autoimmune disorders. You can buy grounding mats to put on your bed to ground you while you are sleeping. Grounding is also excellent for children and pets. I have a grounding mat on my bed and this helped with my fiancée's snoring. I keep one at my desk under my keyboard that keeps me grounded while working.

SEX

Sexual healing is one of the greatest gifts our creator bestowed upon us. Sex (Soul Energy eXchange) is a key ingredient for health and healthy relationships. Sexual healing doesn't only involve intercourse but also includes using eye contact, breathwork, chakra clearing, and acupressure points to bring us closer to our beloved. Done with the intention of passing Soul Energy, sex is an act that increases levels of dopamine, making you feel euphoric. Your orbitofrontal cortex becomes less active, which stops thoughts like judgement, fear, and worry. Of course, there are also the calorie burning benefits. Pro tip from an unprofessional: When creating the space and time for your partner, be luxurious and generous.

SLEEP

Not enough can be said about how the body and mind heals during sleep. The promise of a luxurious sleep along with waking up well-rested and full of energy is often overlooked. Now we lay awake in our beds with our endless mind chatter and endless video options, exhausted.

Exhausted but unrelaxed. Even though I have never had a TV in my bedroom, I now find myself surrounded with cell phone, tablet, and laptop. Next to my bed night table is a bottle of melatonin, CBD, oil, and a good book, but think about this: before electronics, what did people do before sleep?

LAUGHTER

It's no joke: laughter is the best medicine. Why is that? I've heard of people healing themselves through laughter and we all know how good it feels to laugh uncontrollably until it hurts. Is it because while you're laughing you are truly in the present? Science says laughter reduces stress hormones like cortisol and adrenaline and increases the level of health-enhancing hormones, like endorphins and dopamine. Lead with laughter. All great leaders embrace and enjoy mirth, merriment, hilarity, festivity, wit, and pun. Be the first to make everyone laugh and put people at ease.

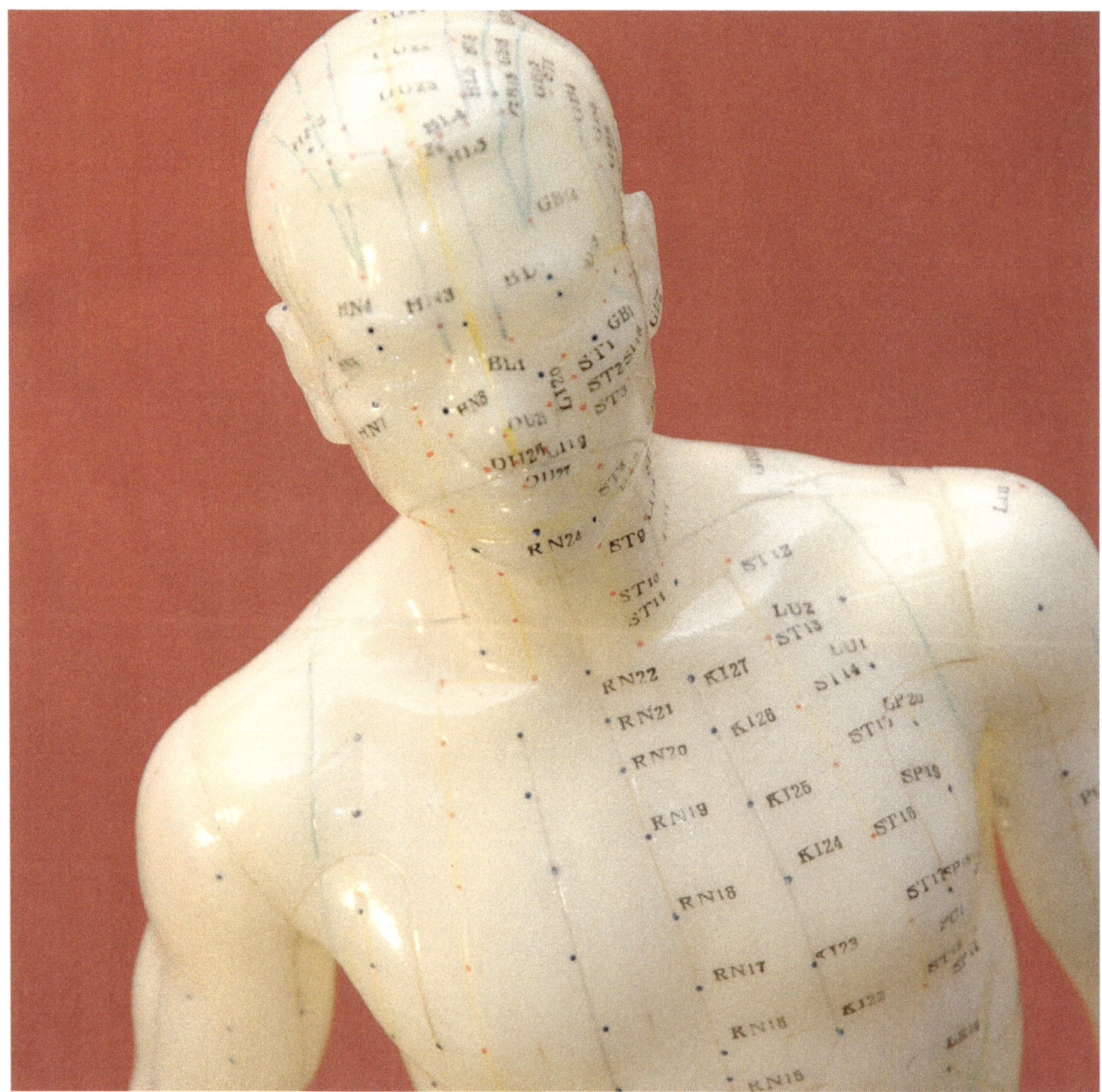

ACUPUNCTURE

Acupuncture is 3000-year-old body healing technology. It works so well and has no side effects. I discovered acupuncture after having terrible shoulder neck pain for weeks. At the ER, my doctor offered pain pills and said I probably "slept wrong": doctor gibberish for "I don't know what's wrong." I took matters into my own hands and searched for a different approach, finding an acupuncturist named Curry Chaudoir, author of Oriental Medicine and You. Curry accurately diagnosed me and knocked out the pain in one treatment. I continue to see Curry twice a month for general health upkeep for libido, post-COVID brain fog, blood pressure, and prostate health.

Acupuncture works with your body's natural healing abilities to increase health and reduce pain. It takes about 45 minutes and it's a relaxing nap for me. I wake up energized and ready to roll. The best part? I keep away from doctors.

NATURE

Getting out in nature is one of the easiest healing modalities and nicest things you can do for yourself and your loved ones. My father grew up in the countryside in Puerto Rico and he was grounded in nature. He was always working in the garden and taking us kids to the forests of the Midwest to hike. When I started bringing my kids into nature, I noticed how much they changed—even after one day! They were grounded and relaxed. The same is true for all of us. Being in nature brings us back to our essential selves. Don't be afraid to be called a tree hugger! It just means you know something others don't.

MAGNESIUM

Do you ever wake up at 3:00 AM? Magnesium is the miracle mineral that will keep you fast asleep. This is my number one sleep-all-night supplement. I find taking magnesium keeps me calm and relaxed even in stressful situations. On the flip side, low levels of magnesium have been linked to diseases including high blood pressure clogged arteries, heart disease, diabetes, and stroke.

SUNSHINE

The laws of thermodynamics dictate we would all be dead without the energy of the sunlight. How did the sun get such a bad rap when its energy is responsible for so much? For people who work inside offices most of the day, the sun is truly magical. It helps us with better sleep by naturally creating melatonin.

Sunlight is especially important for mental health, too, as the sun's rays increase serotonin, which gives you a sense of well-being. Often, those winter blues are caused by decreased levels of serotonin.

Sunlight helps the body make vitamin D which is beneficial for our immune system. A lack of vitamin D is one of the causes of increased illnesses during the winter.

Here's my recommendation: Get out from behind the desk and soak up a few moments of sun! You'll feel better right away.

NUTRITION

Let food be thy medicine and let medicine by thy food. These are the words attributed to the Greek Hippocrates the founder of Western Medicine. Of course, we all been told about eating right but what about food as medicine?

So many drugs are made by synthesizing plant extractions, so it is of course reasonable to enjoy a diet full of benefits to one's health. Having had prostate cancer, I was able to reduce my PSA score through diet. I met a friend during a Vitamin C IV and he suggested lowering PSA through a reduced sugar diet. Not only did I reduce my PSA score I also lost weight and looked better.

While going through Proton therapy I made sure that I was eating foods rich in anti-oxidants like blue berries, pomegranates, strawberries and dark chocolate can keep free radicals at bay and keep you healthy and fit to get over the effects of radiation.

I have never felt better and I have never eaten better than I am now. So what foods are you eating to increase your health?

HEALING

How do you define Healing?

However you define it or however it looks like to you, I invite you to embark on that journey.

Do what works for you, but commit to working on yourself. It just might change your life!

ABOUT THE AUTHOR

Author, speaker, and *Telcom & Data* CEO Ricardo Trinidad has been an entrepreneur as long as he can remember. Raised in a working-class family on Chicago's South Side, his Puerto Rican father and Texan mother led by example through their daily hard work. Trinidad followed suit, "making" jobs for himself to earn extra money.

After completing high school and a few college courses, Trinidad's path led to the tele-communications industry. Employed by an Edison, NJ-based telecom and data company, he was asked to open an office in Chicago. After a few years, Trinidad founded Telcom & Data in his Chicago apartment with $3,000 in savings.

His risk and tenacity paid off. The company grew quickly because of his industry knowledge, the relationships he had built in the field, and his collaborative leadership style.

Twenty-two years later and now headquartered in Milwaukee; Telcom & Data is one of the nation's leading providers of traditional telecommunications equipment.

Trinidad is a sought-after speaker and trainer who particularly enjoys mentoring young people.

www.ingramcontent.com/pod-product-compliance
Lightning Source LLC
Chambersburg PA
CBHW040002290426
43673CB00078B/343